S0-EKM-519

The Divine Speaking

Witness Lee

Living Stream Ministry
Anaheim, California

©1985 Witness Lee

First Edition, 5,000 copies. September 1985.

Library of Congress Catalog
Card Number: 85-81561

ISBN 0-87083-110-0 (hardback)
ISBN 0-87083-111-9 (softback)

Published by

Living Stream Ministry
1853 W. Ball Road, P. O. 2121
Anaheim, CA 92804 U.S.A.

Printed in the United States of America

CONTENTS

CONTENTS

PREFACE

These messages contained in this book concerning the divine speaking were given during a conference in Berkeley, California during the Labor Day weekend of August 30 through September 2, 1985.

Chapter One

THE DIVINE SPEAKING IN GOD'S OLD CREATION AND IN HIS NEW CREATION

Scripture Reading: Heb. 1:1-2a; 11:3a; Gen. 1:3; Psa. 33:9; Num. 11:28-29; John 1:1, 14; 17:7; Mark 1:3; John 14:10b; 5:24; Acts 1:8; 2:3; 14:17-18; 5:42; 8:4; 6:7; 12:24; 19:20; Rom. 10:14; 1 Cor. 14:1, 31

CULTIVATING, PROMOTING, AND BUILDING UP THE HOME MEETINGS

Since last fall the Lord has been leading us to pay our full attention to His up-to-date move, to promote and build up the small meetings in the homes. Since that time I myself have really sold my entire being to this matter. I investigated and I researched to find out what is the most prevailing way to practice the home meetings. Eventually, up to these last few days, I have come to a conclusion: the best way to cultivate and to promote and to build up home meetings is by speaking.

When the New Testament speaks concerning Christian meetings, it always stresses one point—speaking. Paul says, "What is it then, brothers? Whenever you come together, each one has a psalm" (1 Cor. 14:26). What is that? You may say that this is for singing, but Ephesians 5 tells us that psalms, hymns, and spiritual songs are firstly not for singing but for speaking. "Speaking to one another in psalms and hymns and spiritual songs" (Eph. 5:19). The speaking here is with psalms, with poetry. Whether you have a psalm or whether you have a teaching or whether you have a revelation, all are for speaking. If you have a tongue, that is for speaking. If you have an interpretation of tongues, that is also speaking. Furthermore, the manifestation of the Holy Spirit that is given to all the saints is firstly the word of wisdom and secondly the word of knowledge (1 Cor. 12:8). In the New Testament the Christian meetings are full of speaking.

Acts 5:42 shows that in the first period of the church life, those new saints who had just gotten saved on the day of Pentecost met from house to house. In each home of the early believers they met. They met to do what? To be silent? No! In this verse you see two words: preaching and teaching. They met from home to home preaching and teaching. What is preaching? Speaking. What is teaching? Speaking. They did nothing but speak. Whether in preaching or in teaching, they were speaking. Everybody spoke.

Then how about today's Christian meetings? In a big congregation with two thousand attendants, most are not speaking. There is one speaker and this one speaker is a killer. He kills the speaking of all the rest. You may say, "Praise the Lord, in 1966 pray-reading came in. The next year calling on the name of the Lord came in, and from that time in the sharings, in the testimonies, we have had a lot of speakers." I say, "Yes, but all the speakers have become professional." Have you noticed this? If I were to come and stay with you for one week, right away I could find out who are the professional praying people and who are the professional testifying people. A small number have become clergical and the rest, most of them, have all been killed. Their tongues have all been cut off. I have been in Anaheim for years, and I can tell you who are the praying priests in Anaheim. Whenever we have the prayer meeting, mostly those professional praying priests do the praying. In the message meetings, I can always figure out who will testify. We have a number of professional testifiers. Every time that I finish speaking and open the meeting for testimonies, I know to whom the meeting will go. It will go to all those professionals.

There is also another class of professionals—the dumb people. All these brothers come in as professionals to be dumb. They all have learned not to speak. They are the top experts at not speaking. Sometimes I beg them, I charge them, I provoke them to speak, but they are just like pieces of marble. If you were to kick them or beat them, they still would not say anything. They are professionals.

Just a little over twenty years ago a dear one who was meeting with us said to me, "You know today is a modern day. To do anything it has to be professional. So for people to speak in the meetings as a service to God, they must be trained professionals." This is exactly the practice of today's Christianity. They open up the seminaries, collect students, and train them to be professional speakers. Today's Christianity depends upon two things: firstly, organization; and secondly, seminary-trained, professional preachers. If you take these two things away from today's Christianity, all of Christianity will collapse.

Then you may say, "Praise the Lord, in the recovery we don't have these." Do not say this. You have arrangement to replace organization. You say you do not organize, but you arrange a lot. You not only have the chair-arrangers; you have arrangers in every aspect of the church life. You just arrange and arrange. Even if your place does not have that big a number, I do believe you have a lot of arrangements. If you do not arrange, the church collapses. Actually that is organizing, but you just change the term. You see a snake and you say that it is a California trout. Actually it is a snake; you just name it a trout. Do you not have the professional speakers? You do. In the meetings in the recovery we have more professional speakers. We do not have only one speaking; at the end of the speaking we have a number of professional testifiers. We do not want anyone professional. Your faces tell me that you are the professional speakers in the meetings. Or, your appearance tells me that you are the professional non-speakers. So I have discovered that it is hard to have the home meetings.

Recently, when we began to practice the home meetings in Taipei, I suggested not having more than ten in each home meeting. It is best, when you have over ten in the meeting, to divide into two meetings. Then I said that the home meetings should not have any leaders. There should be no human headship. We only have one Head, that is, the unseen Lord Jesus Christ. This practice sounded strange to the saints in Taipei. They began to consider, "We can't do that. How could we have a meeting with just seven or eight? Who would speak? We don't have that many speakers. The church in Taipei has twenty-one halls, and it is a heavy burden already for us to get twenty-one brothers to speak every Sunday morning. If we would divide the entire church in Taipei into 399 meetings we would need 399 speakers. How could we do this? And no leaders? How could seven or eight come together with no leader? How could we practice this?"

Then the report of these two proposals went to the other churches and they tried to follow. Yet the way they followed was not according to my proposal. They followed by arranging some secret leaders. They would fellowship with some saying, "Brother, you know that in your little group there are only young ones. So many are new ones. They don't know anything. You are the only one. You have to bear the responsibility. But we don't mean that you have to be the leader. You should not consider yourself a leader. Don't practice or behave yourself as a leader. Don't be a leader, but be the secret leader and take the lead to speak."

All these considerations and these arrangements cause me to be very concerned. We still arrange for someone to be the speaker. Secretly we ordain one speaker. Most Christians practice their meetings in the way of having one speaker. The others would not speak in the meeting. It is hard to maintain a Christian worship service without a speaker. You need a speaker and the better the speaker is, the more people would attend. Today all the Christian groups are striving and competing to get the best speakers. Today Christianity depends on two things: organization and speakers.

My proposals concerning the home meetings will rescue the churches from oldness and deadness. The way to preserve the churches is to have home meetings with a lot of speaking.

Let me illustrate a home meeting without the adequate speaking. We all come in and sit there in a silent way. I look at you and you look at me. This is the home meeting. Then eventually, because I am the secret leader, I have to say something. I was arranged and I was ordained. I was charged by the elders, so I say, "Brother, did you know that the President got surgery on his nose?" Then you will say, "Yes, that's too bad." Then another says, "No, that's not too bad. That is a kind of healing." Then there is a lot of talking about healings. Eventually we will discuss how to start the home meeting. One would say, "We were charged not to begin the home meeting by calling a hymn." Then another says, "Yes, we were even charged not to begin the home meeting by prayer." Then a third adds, "Yes, I heard we should not begin the home meeting by reading a scripture verse." Then a new one will say, "Then what? It seems quite strange to start a meeting without calling a hymn, without praying, or without reading verses from the Bible. How could we begin the meeting?" Then another says, "I don't agree with this. This is foolish. Is this is a home meeting?" Then what shall we do? Finally we decide to follow the Christianity way. What is the Christianity way? To call and sing a hymn first; then someone prays; then some read the Bible; and then someone gives a message.

Why are we so poor in the meeting? There is no speaking. What can enliven this situation? What can rescue this situation? Speaking! When you come into the meeting, you can say, "Praise the Lord! Amen! Brothers, let me tell you a story. I tell you, I really enjoyed the Lord today. When I was with my wife, she tried to put me down. But, praise the Lord, I prayed for her, and she turned to the Lord, and we had a wonderful time enjoying Christ together." Then another can say, "Oh, I really enjoyed the Lord today. Someone came to my office to complain, so I began speaking to him about Christ. The Triune God takes care of all the complaints. He is our life." Then the next one will speak, "I was going to the campus to preach the gospel. Then I found out that I was really shy. I was afraid to talk to people. So I began praying. I prayed, 'Lord Jesus, You are my boldness.' Then when I came to people in this way, praise the Lord, the Lord was my boldness." Such a meeting full of speaking would be so rich. Bring the rich speaking and don't kill the meeting with a sea story: "This morning I had a difficult time because I realized that I had to catch a flight from work and come all the way to San Francisco. So I felt when I woke up this morning, maybe I wouldn't go to morning watch, but my wife and I considered that I should go to morning watch, so we..." This is too much of a sea story.

We all need to practice speaking all day long. Then when we come to the meeting, we just speak. We should not speak as if we were in a Christianity service. We should not speak in a doctrinal way. Do not speak with a kind of introduction. Just speak. Just speak in an ordinary, common way, so spontaneously. Whenever we are accustomed to opening our mouth in the meetings, we open it in a professional way. But when we talk in our home, we do not speak in this way. We should come to the meeting to talk as we talk in our homes in our daily life. Come together and begin the meeting by speaking.

Humanly speaking, it is hard for several to gather together and sit for five minutes without speaking. This is nearly impossible. Even if they were dumb, they would still try to utter some sounds. It would be hard even for the dumb ones not to speak for several minutes. But it is so strange, even a "miracle," that more than fifty Christians can sit in a prayer meeting without speaking. The meeting may begin at 7:30, but by 7:35 the fifty are still sitting there without speaking. This is a "miracle." Too often this happens. I do not know why. Some may appreciate this situation saying, "My, these Christians are marvelous people. They can sit there without speaking for a quarter of an hour. Surely they are the trained people. They are so silent that you can hear the falling of a pin on the floor. They are so quiet, so silent, without speaking." It is hard for me to tolerate such a situation or the deadness and oldness, without any speaking.

Let us come back to the Bible. The Bible is *the* book. We all know what a book is. A book is just full of speaking. If you do not have any speaking in a book, that could not be a book. Hebrews 1:1-2 says, "In many portions and in many ways, God, having spoken of old to the fathers in the prophets, has at the last of these days spoken to us in the Son." God spoke in old times, here and there, in this part and in that part. He spoke in many parts, on many occasions. He spoke through the prophets. Then in the New Testament He spoke in a Person. You have to realize that this Person was firstly individual. Eventually, this Person becomes corporate. The strange thing is this: God's speaking in the Old Testament was through the prophets. But Hebrews 1:1 does not say that today God's speaking is through the apostles. It says that God's speaking today is not through any channels, but in a Person. God today speaks in a Person, and this Person today has been increased to be a corporate person. This Person includes all the apostles, and all the members of this Person's Body. Today God is speaking through one Person, a corporate Person. Today He is still speaking. In this message He is speaking through me. But it is not actually through me, but through the Person of Christ. This Person is an enlarged Person, a corporate Person. Today God is speaking in this Person.

THE DIVINE SPEAKING IN THE OLD TESTAMENT

What the Bible reveals concerning the divine speaking in the old creation is firstly seen in Genesis chapter one. The Bible tells us clearly that the old creation was created by God's speaking. Genesis 1:3 says, "And God said, Let there be light: and there was light." This was done by speaking. For this reason Hebrews 11:3 tells us, "By faith we understand that the universe has been framed by the word of God." "And God said, Let there be a firmament... and it was so. ...And God said, Let the waters under the heaven be gathered together...and it was so" (Gen. 1:6, 7, 9). Psalm 33:9 says that when God spoke, it was done. When God spoke, that was it! God did not use any gimmicks, any messages, any channels to create the universe. God created the universe only by speaking! He spoke and it was.

Following this, in the Old Testament for quite a long time, there is not much record of God's speaking. Of course, He spoke to Noah, but not so much. Then He spoke to Abraham, but even to Abraham He did not speak so much. But when Moses came, he became the top speaker of God. God used him to speak. We all know that the first five books, the Pentateuch, were written by Moses. The law, the ordinances, the regulations, and all those types were all written by him. In other words, these were spoken by Moses and through Moses. Numbers 11 records that the responsibility among God's people was too heavy for Moses alone. At that time, God took the Spirit, who was upon Moses, and put the Spirit upon the seventy elders (Num. 11:25). All the elders began to prophesy. At the same time, the Spirit rested upon two of them who remained in the camp. They also began to speak as prophets. When Moses' attendant, Joshua, heard this, he reported to Moses and begged him, "My lord Moses, forbid them." Moses replied, "Enviest thou for my sake? would God that all Jehovah's people were prophets, and that Jehovah would put his Spirit upon them" (Num. 11:28-29). That indicated that God's desire was to make all His people prophets. That was in the old creation.

THE DIVINE SPEAKING IN THE NEW TESTAMENT

Now we come to God's speaking in the new creation. How was the new creation made? It was made by speaking. First, the entire God was the Word. This means that the entire God was a speaking. "In the beginning was the Word...and the Word was God" (John 1:1). This Word became incarnated to be a man, and that man was just God's speaking. The man Jesus was God's Word. In other words, He was God's speaking. He told us that He was one with the Father; He was in the Father and the Father was in Him; and the word He spoke was God's working in Him (John 14:10). Then He said, "He who hears My word and believes Him Who sent Me has eternal life, and will not come into judgement, but has passed out of death into life" (John 5:24). This is the new creation brought into being by speaking.

Before the day of Pentecost came, the Lord Jesus told His disciples, "You shall receive power when the Holy Spirit has come upon you, and you shall be My witnesses." (Acts 1:8) This means, "You shall be My speaking people to speak for Me." We all know what a witness is. A witness is a speaking person, one who testifies by speaking. Then the day of Pentecost came. What happened at that time? Tongues of fire came down. We all know that tongues are for speaking. On the day of Pentecost tongues came upon all the believers and they began to speak. It is no wonder that right away after the day of Pentecost, three thousand, and then five thousand, all met in their homes, speaking, preaching, and teaching. Everyone spoke. They did not need to worry about their home meeting, whether they would have speakers or not. Everyone spoke. Everyone witnessed. Everyone preached. Everyone taught. Everyone!

Then Acts says, "The word of God grew and multiplied." The same kind of phrase is repeated in Acts three times (6:7;

12:24; 19:20). How did the word of God grow? It was by speaking! In Jerusalem when the great persecution came, all the three thousand and five thousand were scattered. Only the apostles were left there in Jerusalem. The scattered ones went out to preach the word, to speak the word by the way of preaching! They all went out to speak, to speak, to speak, to every village. When the eunuch from Ethiopia was riding in a chariot, Philip was told to speak to him. This was an example of speaking. It was not in congregations nor in arranged meetings. Rather, everywhere they just spoke.

Eventually, Paul said nearly the same thing as Moses did. Moses said, "Would God that all Jehovah's people were prophets, and that Jehovah would put his Spirit upon them"(Num. 11:29). Likewise, Paul said, "For you can all prophesy one by one" (1 Cor. 14:31). It is a poor situation that most of the Christian people today understand the word "prophesy" to mean to predict. But when Moses used the Hebrew word for "prophesy," his intention was not to indicate "to predict." Even he himself did not predict much! In all his five books how many predictions are there? Very few. But his writing, that is his speaking, was altogether the speaking forth of God. He was speaking for God and he was speaking God! He predicted little. It was the same with Isaiah, Jeremiah, and Ezekiel. Their books actually contain very few predictions, but rather are full of speaking forth God, speaking for God, and speaking God directly. This was the Old Testament prophecy: not much prediction, but full of speaking forth of God, speaking for God, and speaking God directly. It is the same way with the Greek word in the New Testament. Prophecy in New Testament Greek means a kind of speaking of God. You speak God forth, you speak Christ out, you speak Christ to people, you speak for Christ. This is prophecy. To prophesy is mainly to speak for Christ, to speak Christ forth, to speak Christ out. To prophesy is to speak God, to speak Christ, to speak the divine interest, to speak the things concerning Christ and God, and to speak forth, speak out, and speak for God.

We all need to practice prophesying every day from morning to evening. We need to practice this kind of speaking for Christ, this kind of speaking forth of Christ, and this kind of speaking out Christ, speaking Christ all the day long. "This is my story, this is my song, speaking my Savior all the day long!" When we are accustomed to speaking, we come to the meeting and just speak. We have a lot of things to speak concerning Christ. Then spontaneously we will have home meetings that are enlivened, enriched, strengthened, and refreshing. They will be made new, attractive, and attracting. They will be full of power and strength to hold people.

Let us all come to the meeting to revolutionize the meeting by speaking! Speaking spontaneously. Speaking Christ. Speaking for Christ. Speaking forth Christ. Speaking out Christ. Speaking Christ to everybody. If when you come to a home meeting, you see that no one is there, you can still speak. Speak Christ to the books! "Books, let me tell you, you don't have a spirit, but I do. You cannot take Christ, but I can! You cannot recieve Christ, but I can! You cannot enjoy Christ, but I can! You know, books, I have enjoyed Christ the whole day today!" No one has come in yet, but the meeting starts with just you yourself. Such a speaking will revolutionize the meeting.

The psalmist in Psalm 19 says, "The heavens declare the glory of God and the firmament sheweth his handiwork." Even the heavens speak! Why do we not speak? We have been created, regenerated, and made His witnesses. We are His witnesses. We have to speak! Do not talk about anything else. Just talk about Christ. Do not talk about the weather. Speak, speak, all the time speak Christ. Then you will be a prophet. So Paul says, "You can all prophesy one by one" (1 Cor. 14:31). You all can! So we all have to learn how to revolutionize our meetings by speaking.

God created the old creation by speaking, and that

creation was carried on by God's people speaking God. Moses was a typical example. He desired that all God's people would be such speakers, prophets speaking God, to carry on the old creation. Then the new creation was created, again by God's word. We all have been made witnesses to speak for God. Paul says that you all can be a speaking one, a prophet speaking God, speaking forth God, speaking for God. You all can do this one by one. This is God's word! So, dear saints, if we are going to promote and build up the home meetings, there is no other way but by speaking.

CHAPTER TWO

THE DIVINE SPEAKING IN OUR DAILY LIFE, MINISTRY, AND MEETINGS

Scripture Reading: Acts 1:8; 8:4-5; Eph. 5:18-22; 2 Tim. 4:1-5; Acts 5:42; 1 Cor. 12:2-3, 9; 14:1, 4, 26, 31

We have seen in the previous chapter that God's desire has always been that all His people, in both the Old and New Testaments would be a speaking people. In this chapter we will cover a number of verses concerning the divine speaking in our daily life, in the ministry, and in our meetings.

WITNESSES OF THE LIVING CHRIST

In Acts 1:8, the Lord Jesus told the disciples, "But you shall receive power when the Holy Spirit has come upon you, and you shall be My witnesses both in Jerusalem, and in all Judea and Samaria, and unto the remotest part of the earth." In this verse the crucial point is, "You shall be My witnesses." Witnesses are speakers. We have to realize that as believers we all have been made the witnesses of the living Christ. When the Lord Jesus spoke this, He was speaking in resurrection. He was not only the incarnated Christ who lived on this earth in His flesh, but He was the Christ who passed through incarnation, human living, crucifixion, and who entered into resurrection. Not many days after this word was spoken the Lord Jesus ascended into heaven. Ten days after His ascension, He poured Himself out as the Spirit of power economically upon His disciples. Then they received the power and were made His witnesses to speak concerning Him. What would they speak? Surely they would speak that this Christ is God, and that this Christ as God was incarnated. Perhaps Peter would say, "I saw Him. When He was a man living on this earth, I accompanied Him all the way from Galilee to Samaria, to Judea, and to Jerusalem. I ate with Him, and I stayed with Him. I lived with Him for three and a half years. I was with Him!" They would continue to tell people, "We saw how He was crucified on the cross, how His blood was shed, and how He was buried. Then on the third day, early in the morning, we went to His tomb and saw that the tomb was empty! The angels there told us that He had resurrected from the tomb! We saw this! Then in the evening He came to us. He showed us His physical body in resurrection with the nail prints. After that He stayed with us, appearing and disappearing for forty days. He charged us to wait until we received power from on high, and we got it! On the mount of Olives we saw Him ascend into the heavens. There the angels told us that He would come back." No doubt, those disciples were speaking Christ in this way. They were witnessing the living One. They were not speaking doctrine. They were not speaking law. They were not speaking prophecy. They were not speaking types, or proverbs, or psalms. They were speaking Christ, a living Person! Their speaking was concerning His being God, His incarnation, His living on this earth, His being crucified, His resurrection, His staying with them in those forty days, and His ascension to heaven. Surely they spoke all these aspects concerning Christ. They spoke nothing but Christ, Christ, Christ, Christ in every aspect.

On the day of Pentecost Peter delivered the first message of the New Testament. This message is recorded in Acts 2. Peter spoke just Christ, telling the Jews, "The very Jesus whom you crucified is the One God raised up! You put Him to death, but God came in to raise Him up, even to uplift Him to the heavens!" Just by that one speaking, three thousand believed and were baptized. Then they began to meet, not only in the temple, but also from home to home. In their homes they preached and they taught. They preached Jesus and they taught Jesus.

SPEAKING CHRIST WITH THE HYMNS

In our home meetings we also need to preach and teach Jesus. We all have to speak! But many of us would not know what to speak. For this reason I would like to present to you the materials for your speaking. In our hymnal we have 1,080 hymns. We collected all the best hymns from the Christian writings. From more than ten thousand hymns we only selected about eight hundred. After the selection, I did my best to classify them into a table of contents for the hymnal. I would ask the young people to study it. This table occupies four and a half pages with thirty categories of hymns. In these thirty categories there are more than four hundred items. Within the category of Experience of Christ there are thirty-two items. These items are the riches of Christ. In the category of meetings we were only able to collect hymns in three sections. Due to the shortage of hymns in this category I did my best to write the few hymns comprising the sections of Christ as the Center, Exhibiting Christ, Exercising the Spirit, and Functioning. Hymn 863 is on Christ as the center of the meetings:

> In daily walk and in our meetings too,
> Christ is the center, Christ is everything;
> 'Tis not for form nor doctrine good and true,
> But 'tis for Christ alone we're gathering.
>
> Christ is the way and Christ the light of life,
> In Him we walk and by Him we are led;
> Christ is the living water and the food;
> Of Him we drink and we with Him are fed.

Christ is the truth, 'tis Him we testify,
Christ is the life, 'tis Him we minister;
Christ is the Lord, 'tis Him we magnify,
Christ is the Head, and we exalt Him here.

Christ is the All in all to God and man—
With Him both we and God are satisfied;
Christ, the reality within the Church—
By Him are life and numbers multiplied.

By all the hymns and prayers we offer here,
Christ the reality we would express;
All the activities in fellowship—
Christ thus in operation manifest.

'Tis in His Name we meet, in Spirit act,
With nothing in our mind to formalize;
'Tis by His pow'r we pray, in unction praise,
And with Himself in spirit exercise.

All things forgetting, cleaving unto Christ,
Applying Him until maturity;
Let us count everything but loss for Him,
For Him, our All in all, eternally!

With just this one hymn in your hand, you have a lot to speak! This hymn is a key to open up the mine for you to dig out all the rich items. Do not say you have nothing to speak in the meetings. You have a lot to speak. Just open to this one hymn. The young saints should not wait to let the older ones preside over, to pastor, the home meetings. We all have a lot to speak concerning Christ. Just turn to Hymn 863 and begin to read and speak, "'In daily walk and in our meetings too, Christ is the center.' Saints, do you know that Christ is the center of our daily walk, and the center of our meeting tonight?" Then the meeting will be very much enriched. We do not need to merely sing the hymn, but even more we need to read and speak it. Ephesians 5:18-19 says, "Be filled in spirit, speaking to one another in psalms and hymns and spiritual songs."

According to our natural, religious concept, songs and hymns are only good for singing. In Christianity I never heard songs, hymns, and psalms spoken in the meetings. But in the New Testament, we are told that the way to be filled in our spirit is by speaking psalms, hymns, and songs. Psalms are the longest pieces, hymns are shorter, and songs are the shortest ones. All these are firstly for speaking, then for singing.

We have to learn to speak the riches of Christ in hymns such as Hymn 864 which begins:

> Whene'er we meet with Christ endued,
>   The surplus of His plenitude
> We offer unto God as food,
>   And thus exhibit Christ.

By what way do we offer Christ to God? We offer Him to God by our speaking to God. This is prayer. However, many times when we pray, it seems that in our prayer we are teaching God. That is absolutely wrong. The most precious prayer is to present Christ to God. Speak Him to God; this is the best prayer.

The hymn continues, "Let us exhibit Christ." To meet is to just have an exhibition of Christ. We exhibit Christ by speaking one to another in hymns, psalms, and songs. The content of our speaking must be the incarnated, crucified, resurrected, and ascended Christ with all His attributes. He is the subject. He is the center. He is God's centrality and universality. He is the reality of our living. We just have to speak Him in many, many items. We present Him to God by speaking Him to God. We exhibit Him to the meeting ones by speaking Him to the meeting ones, by speaking to one another. We have a lot of riches of Christ to speak. We need to learn to speak Christ to God and to speak Christ to one another.

In Ephesians 5:18-19 Paul says, "And do not be drunk with wine, in which is dissipation, but be filled in spirit, speaking to one another in psalms and hymns and spiritual songs, singing and psalming with your heart to the Lord." We are to be filled with the Triune God as the all-inclusive, consummated Spirit in our spirit. This filling occurs, not by our speaking in the common, worldly language, but by speaking to one another in psalms, hymns, and spiritual songs. In our hymnal there are many good hymns full of the truth. Every hymn, especially those written by us, is a good message full of the riches of Christ. For example, Hymn 501 describes how Christ was the infinite God in eternity, who as God's radiant expression became a finite man, limited in time. As the very expression of God, He died for us to accomplish redemption in His flesh. Then He became a life-giving Spirit to be one with us. We must learn to speak Christ with the hymns. I believe these hymnals are good for having our home meetings. Every meeting use a hymn in a living way.

SPEAKING CHRIST AS THE HEAVENLY LANGUAGE

Just as we would have to study, translate, read, and write in learning a new language we all need to practice speaking the heavenly, spiritual and Christly language. In this language there is only one word: Christ. In Revelation 1:8 He is even the Alpha and the Omega, the first and last letter of the New Testament language. This indicates that He is all the letters of the alphabet. Revelation 19:3 also says that His name is called the Word of God. Christ is the letter. Christ is the word. Christ is the phrase. Christ is the clause. Christ is the sentence, the paragraph, the chapter, and the whole book.

SPEAKING CHRIST TO OTHERS IN A LIVING WAY

Acts 8:1 tells us that all the thousands of new believers were scattered throughout Judea and Samaria as a result of a great persecution. Only the apostles remained in Jerusalem. Those who were scattered preached the good news of the word wherever they went. Although these believers had been saved only a short time, when they were scattered they spoke Jesus. Had they learned as much as we have? Many of us have been in the trainings for years. We have heard a lot. In the past eleven and a half years I have put out over twelve hundred Life-study messages on the twenty-seven books of the New Testament. These printed messages comprise over twelve thousand pages. Most of us have a set of the printed Life-studies on our shelves. We have a lot. Those scattered ones in Acts 8, however, had heard very little about Christ, yet they went out to speak Him. Prior to being scattered they had only heard Peter's messages in Acts 2 through 5. In all of Peter's messages Peter did not speak anything about being saved from hell and going to heaven. What Peter spoke was altogether the resurrected Christ: "Let all the house of Israel know assuredly that God has made Him both Lord and Christ—this Jesus whom you crucified" (Acts 2:36). This was Peter's speaking, and surely those scattered ones had learned just to speak the same thing. Wherever they went they spoke Christ.

Dear saints, now we are in the Lord's recovery and I do believe that now is the time for the Lord to carry out His up-to-date move. All of us in the Lord's recovery have to speak Christ in our daily life to our parents, our children, our cousins, and our in-laws. We all owe so much to our relatives. Try to write a list of all the names of your relatives. Among these names maybe twenty percent are saved, and the rest are remaining in unbelief. They need your speaking. All of your relatives need the real help rendered by your speaking of Christ. Do not preach in a religious way, but speak Christ to your relatives in a living way. Speak to your father. Speak to your mother. Speak to your aunt. Speak to your uncle. Speak to your brother. Even if both you and your brother are Christians, you still need to speak one to another. Let your parents hear your speaking. Do not talk about computers, physics, or mathematics, but only Christ. He is the unique treasure! Speak about Jesus, Christ, the life-giving Spirit, the all-inclusive, processed Triune God. Your parents would marvel at such a speaking.

Continue to speak Christ every day. All human beings today need Christ, yet we need to speak to them. Speak in a living way, in a practical way, according to your experience of Him. Speak in your office, at the coffee break, at your lunch break, at least five minutes every day, five days a week, four weeks a month. At least twenty times monthly you could speak Christ to them.

In the past few years many of us felt that we could not speak to others due to the defamation of the opposers. We should not take this excuse any longer. Forget about all the defamations. We just need to speak Christ to others. Nothing is so sweet, so fresh, so fragrant as Jesus. We have to speak Him.

PREACHING THE WORD IN SEASON AND OUT OF SEASON

In 2 Timothy 4:2, Paul charged Timothy to "preach the word; be ready in season and out of season." When I was studying this verse, I checked with myself as to what word Paul charged Timothy to preach. That helped me to go back to the preceding chapter. Chapter four verse 1 is surely a continuation of Paul's thought at the end of chapter three. In the last three verses of chapter three Paul says, "And that from a babe you have known the sacred writings, which are able to make you wise unto salvation through faith which is in Christ Jesus. All Scripture is God-breathed and profitable for teaching, for reproof, for correction, for instruction in righteousness, that the man of God may be complete, fully equipped for every good work." From these verses we can realize that the word Paul charged Timothy to preach was the word in the sacred writings of the Scriptures that Timothy had known from a babe. We all have to get into the Word, into the Scriptures.

The charge of the Apostle Paul to Timothy was based upon Timothy's knowledge of the Bible. If he had not known the Bible, what kind of word could he have preached? We must preach the word that we have learned from the Word of God. This is what the early believers did in Acts 5:42 when they met from house to house "teaching and bringing the good news of Jesus as the Christ." In the home meetings they taught and preached what they had learned concerning Christ.

Paul charged Timothy to be ready "in season and out of season," to preach the word. Many times we say that now is not the time to speak; that it is out of season. That is the right time for us to speak. We all must speak out of season. I surely treasure all the young saints and desire to rescue them from the pastoral system. The young ones who are still in school have the most people around them. Every school is a big fishing pond full of fish. This is an environment arranged by God for speaking to others. Students always enjoy listening to their classmates much more than to their teachers or parents. We have to learn to catch these fish by speaking Christ to them. We have to be made the fishers of men, bringing people to Christ and to the home meetings. For this, I do not trust in any human arrangement, but in the young saints' acting, behaving, working, endeavoring, and struggling to contact their fellow students. If we would do this, within a short time many would be baptized and added to the churches.

SPEAKING IN THE HOLY SPIRIT
FOR THE BUILDING UP OF THE CHURCH

In 1 Corinthians chapter twelve, Paul refers to the matter of speaking in the meetings. In verse 2 he reminds the Corinthians, "You know that when you were of the nations, you were led away to dumb idols, however you were led." The worship of dumb idols had made them a dumb people. Because the object of their worship was a dumb idol, their worshipping made them a dumb people.

But now the Corinthian brothers were different. They were not worshipping the dumb idols any more. They were worshipping the living God, who is the speaking God. This speaking God is just the speaking Spirit, who is the Spirit of God, who is also the Holy Spirit. Therefore, in verse 3 Paul says, "No one speaking in the Spirit of God says, Jesus is accursed; and no one can say, Lord Jesus, except in the Holy Spirit." I like these two phrases, "in the Spirit of God" and "in the Holy Spirit." "In" means that we all have been put into this Spirit. If you are not in Him, if you are not in the Holy Spirit, how could you speak something in the Holy Spirit? Can we all say that we are in the Holy Spirit? Be careful about my question. I do not ask is the Holy Spirit within us. We all have the assurance to say that the Holy Spirit is in us, but are we in the Holy Spirit? Doctrinally we may say yes. We have to know that the Spirit being in us is the essential aspect of the Spirit, and that our being in the Spirit is economical. I believe that many of us already know that the Spirit on the one hand is a drink to us, and on the other hand is clothing to us. Drinking is something within; clothing is something upon us. The drinking water is in us, and we are in the clothing. If the Holy Spirit is in us, then are we in the Spirit? Some Pentecostal people may say, "No! You are not in the Spirit yet. You need a baptism with the Holy Ghost. You need to get into the Spirit. You need to pray and fast and learn how to turn your jaw to speak in tongues. Then you will have the baptism of the Holy Spirit and you will be in the Spirit." In verse 3 Paul did not say that no can speak in tongues except in the Holy Spirit. I cannot find such a word in the Bible. Paul said no one can say, Lord Jesus. Can you say, "Lord Jesus"? If so you are in the Holy Spirit! Go and tell this to your relatives, friends, and colleagues. We do have 1 Corinthians 12:3 as a solid ground to say, and to say with assurance, that we are in the Holy Spirit. We do not need to speak in a strange tongue, but rather just say, "O Lord Jesus," and we are in the Spirit.

When we come to the meetings, we need to practice speaking this way in the Holy Spirit. Do not stand up in the meeting and say, "Brothers and sisters, I have been very weak in these last two weeks. I'm still weak. You can see how weak I am." This is terrible. When you stand up in the meeting to speak, stand up in this way, "Brothers and sisters let me tell you, I am no longer weak! I am empowered in the One who empowers me, so I can do everything. Formerly I could not submit myself to my husband. Now it's easy for me to do it. I am the top wife. Hallelujah, brothers." This is the best speaking. In every locality, some saints have learned to be "professional" priests praying whenever the church comes together for the prayer meeting. These dear ones are the "professionals" to pray in the meetings. In the same way, some saints have become "professional" at giving a testimony at the end of the message meetings. I use the word "professional" in a positive sense. That is, we all have to learn to be the "professional" speakers speaking in the Holy Spirit.

When we open our mouth to speak, we need to open our mouth with the Spirit. Some may say, "It is very hard to attend the meetings of the local church. I have to bear a lot of burden, learning of this and of that. But to be a member in today's Christianity is altogether a kind of relaxation. I have been busy working hard at the office, or going to classes during the week. On Sundays, I just like to go to church to relax. The choir will do the singing. The assistant pastor will pray. The pastor will speak, or perhaps an evangelist who has just returned from South Africa. After an hour and thirty minutes I will give some gift then go home. I enjoy that I don't have to labor. But to be a member in the local church I have to learn how to be a professional speaker. To speak, 'O Lord Jesus' is too hard. Everybody does it, so if I don't do it, I get exposed. Therefore I have to do something to pretend." My intention is to show you that the Lord today needs a recovery. Look at the situation which has been existing on

this earth for twenty centuries. In Matthew 16:18 the Lord
said He would build His church. Where is the building?
Who affords a chance for Jesus Christ as the Head of the
Body to build the church? Probably we are also quite busy,
being occupied, usurped, by so many schedules, activities,
and movements without Christ.

I would like to remind you of something Dr. A. W. Tozer
once said. He put out an article entitled, "The Waning
Authority of Christ in the Churches." In that article his
burden was to point out that today Jesus Christ has almost
no authority at all among the groups that call themselves
by His name. Christian workers may come together to talk
about serving Christ yet if Christ were to come in, they
would not know Him. This indicates that He is not among
them, He is not in their midst. He is outside of them. This
corresponds with the word the Lord spoke in the epistle to
the church in Laodicea (Rev. 3:14-22). In verse 20, the Lord
Jesus is standing outside of the door of that church,
knocking. This is the situation of today. There is no way,
no possibility, no capacity, no space, for Him to come in
to do any kind of building. This is why the Lord is here
to carry out His recovery, and this is why we have such
a burden.

In Matthew 18:17 the church is referred to again. Here
the church is not the universal church, but the local
church. In the local church, two or three meet together into
the Lord's name. The name denotes a Person. That means
two or three are gathered into Him. Whenever in the home
meetings two or three are gathered into Christ, that is the
time for Him to build up the church. It is in the local
church that there is the possibility of dealings. Even the
sinning ones get dealt with there. Now you can see that
actually the practical building of the church is not in
chapter sixteen. The building that is mentioned, predicted,
and prophesied in chapter sixteen will be carried out today
in chapter eighteen, in the local churches where two or
three meet together into Him. The big congregation can

never build people up. We need the small meetings, small to such an extent that only two or three come together. In such a meeting there is the possibility for Him to build up the church.

Today what we are stressing is something up-to-date of the Lord's move and His recovery. He has to recover this unique thing. This is why I treasure the small meetings. There is no other way to build up the church but by all of us learning to speak Christ, to speak for Christ, and to speak forth Christ. We must speak in our daily life, in our office, in our school, in our family, in our ministry, and especially in the small meetings.

It is no wonder that Paul stressed this matter of speaking so much. In 1 Corinthians 12:7 Paul says that the manifestation of the Holy Spirit is given, not primarily as miraculous things, but as a word of wisdom and a word of knowledge. The word of wisdom is the word concerning Christ as the deeper things of God predestined by God for our portion. This refers to Christ in a deeper experience as revealed in 1 Corinthians 2:6-10. The word of knowledge is the word that imparts the definition, description, and understanding of Christ as God's everything. But we need to know this. We need the word of knowledge concerning Christ's riches, such as His being our righteousness, our wisdom, our power, our justification, our sanctification, and our redemption, and we need the word of wisdom concerning the depths of Christ. We need to speak these things. We need the word of wisdom to speak the depths of Christ, and we need the word of knowledge to describe all the rich aspects of Christ. In 1 Corinthians 14 Paul says, "Desire earnestly spiritual gifts, but rather that you may prophesy," that you may speak for God (v. 1). In verse 4 Paul says, "He who speaks in a tongue builds up himself, but he who prophesies builds up the church." To build up others and to build up the church we need to prophesy, to speak forth Christ. Then in verse 26 Paul says, "Whenever you come together, each one has a psalm." This corresponds with Ephesians 5:18-19, "Be filled in spirit, speaking to one another in psalms." When we come together we should have a psalm for speaking Christ, or a teaching telling people the things concerning Christ, or a revelation, the word of wisdom, to unveil the depths of Christ. We have to do all for the building up of others and of the church.

All these verses show us that the way to meet, especially in the small home meetings, is to speak Christ. Learn to speak Christ. To practice this present move of the Lord needs a lot of learning. I do not expect that we could get this done successfully in a short time. I rather would expect initially to have a failure. To be successful in anything, there first must be some failures. If within the coming three years we could have the home meetings fully built up, this might be the greatest mercy and grace that the Lord would give us. Pray for this. I just present this to you and to your discernment. I hope that you all could have the best discerning ability in your spirit that you would say, "Praise the Lord, this is no doubt the Lord's up-to-date move to accomplish, to carry out, His recovery for the fullfilling of His eternal purpose in building up the church."

CHAPTER THREE

THE DIVINE SPEAKING
IN THE HOLY SPIRIT
BY THE SPIRIT OF FAITH

Scripture Reading: 1 Cor. 12:3; 2 Cor. 4:7-14; 5:7; 1 Cor. 14:4, 19

What we are considering here, the divine speaking, is quite crucial to our Christian experience. So many riches in the Bible have all been lost or neglected by Christians throughout the centuries. Even up until 500 years ago, that great item of God's economy, justification by faith, was lost. It was through the Reformers under the leadership of Martin Luther that this item was recovered. The divine speaking also has been, and still is, missed, lost, and neglected by Christians today. This is why there is the need of the Lord's recovery.

As we have seen in the previous chapter, all Christians have been made the witnesses of Christ. As witnesses we must be persons speaking. We must be speaking for Christ, telling something of Christ to others. A dumb person could never be a witness. We must be speakers, those speaking clearly, adequately, and definitely for the One we witness. I hope that we all would go out to speak. For example, we can speak something to our relatives. We can tell them something concerning Christ's death, something concerning Christ's resurrection, and something concerning the Body of Christ, and the local church. In this matter Christianity has altogether missed the mark. We must come back to the Bible and mine the store of the divine riches. Then we will have so much to speak.

SPEAKING IN THE HOLY SPIRIT
The Consummation of the Triune God

The divine speaking is in the Holy Spirit. To be in the Holy Spirit is not a small thing. Who is the Holy Spirit? Throughout the last twenty centuries there have been many debates concerning the Spirit. Even less than four hundred years ago, Christians still did not understand the Holy Spirit to be a Person. In translating the New Testament, the King James translators did not use the personal pronouns he, him, or his with regard to the Spirit; they still used it, its, and itself. This indicated that they did not consider the Holy Spirit to be a Person. According to this concept, the Father in the Trinity is a Person, and the Son is also a Person, but the Spirit is not. They considered the Spirit just as a means, a channel, or an instrument by which the Father and the Son accomplish something. In the middle part of last century, the British Brethren, mostly under the teaching of John Nelson Darby, saw that this was wrong. In his *New Translation* of the New Testament, Darby began to change the pronouns referring to the Spirit to the personal pronouns he, him, or his.

In the first part of this century when the Lord raised us up, we made a very strong decision not to be influenced by anything of the past. We appreciated all the Western missionaries who went to China, and we thanked the Lord for them, because they brought three treasures to us: the name of the Lord Jesus, the gospel, and the Bible. We decided just to take these three things and nothing else. We made a strong decision that we must start to have something purely and absolutely according to the pure word of the Bible. That was the start of the Lord's recovery in China.

In this way we began to study the Bible. I myself have been studying this crucial item, the Triune God, for sixty years. This is my major. Of course, it is not only I who like to talk about the Triune God; the Bible speaks much about the Triune God, especially in the New Testament. I discovered by thorough study that nearly every book of the New Testament is constituted with the divine Trinity. For example, Matthew at its conclusion says, "Go therefore and disciple all the nations, baptizing them into the name of the Father and of the Son and of the Holy Spirit" (Matt. 28:19). Likewise, 1 Peter says that we were chosen by the Father, sanctified by the Holy Spirit, and sprinkled with the blood of Jesus Christ (1 Pet. 1:1-2). The conclusion of 2 Corinthians says, "The grace of the Lord Jesus Christ, and the love of God, and the fellowship of the Holy Spirit be with you all" (2 Cor. 13:14). This is the divine Trinity.

After sixty years of study, I came to this conclusion: the Father is the source, the Son is the embodiment of the Triune God, and the Spirit is the realization of the Triune God. Now I would improve this a little more by saying that the Spirit is the consummation of the Triune God. The Father is the source, the Son is the embodiment, and the Spirit is the consummation of the Triune God. The the entire Triune God, is consummated in the Spirit. Hallelujah! Genesis 1:1 and 2 say, "In the beginning God created the heaven and the earth...And the Spirit of God brooded over the face of the waters" (Heb.). God created, and the Spirit of God brooded to produce for God's creation. But the last chapter of the Bible, as the conclusion of the sixty-six books says, "The Spirit and the bride say, Come" (Rev. 22:17). This verse says, "The Spirit", not God, nor even the Spirit of God, not even the Holy Spirit. This indicates that the Spirit as the consummation of the processed and dispensed Triune God is the Husband, and the bride, as the aggregate of the regenerated and transformed, tripartite men, is the wife. Who is the Holy Spirit? He is not only the Spirit of God, He is the consummation of the entire Triune God.

I have a strong base to speak in this way. When the Son came, He did not come alone. He came with the Father (John 16:32). When He was living on the earth, His Father was all the time with Him. Even when He was conceived in the womb of the human virgin, God the Father was with Him. He never left the Father. It is impossible to separate Him from the Father. No doubt, the Son and the Father are distinct. Just by the titles we can see that one is the Father and one is the Son. But there is no separation. In John 14:10, He said, "Do you not believe that I am in the Father, and the Father is in Me? The words which I speak to you, I do not speak from Myself; but the Father Who abides in Me, He does His works." While He was speaking there, He told His disciples that He was at that time in the Father, and the Father was in Him. He was never separated from the Father. When He went to the cross, He died there, and the Father was with Him. He was, and still is, the very embodiment of the Triune God. This is proven in Colossians 2:9: "For in Him dwells all the fullness of the Godhead [the Triune God] bodily." Then at the end of His earthly ministry, He told His disciples that He would ask the Father to give them another Comforter. John 14 through 16 reveal that this other Comforter is just the realization of Himself (14:17-20; 16:12-14). Therefore, this Comforter is called the Spirit of reality. We may say that the Spirit of reality is the realization of the Son, Christ, as the embodiment of the Triune God.

In John 16:15 He tells us that all that the Father has, has been given over to Him. All that the Son is and has, has been realized in the Spirit. Then the Spirit comes to us to make all this real. Whatever the Father is, is embodied in the Son, and whatever the Son embodies is realized in the Spirit. Who then is the Spirit? He is the realization, the consummation of the entire Triune God. If you receive Him, you receive the Triune God. If you receive Him, you receive Him with the Son and with the Father. If you receive Him, you receive all the Three, the Father, the Son and the Spirit.

Therefore, when we speak in the Holy Spirit we speak in the Triune God. We must realize this and declare it. It would even be good for us to become excited and jump up, declaring, "We speak in the Triune God!"

Baptized into the Holy Spirit

Our being in the Triune God corresponds with the baptism in Matthew 28:19. When we were baptized, we were baptized into the Triune God. It is not too much to say that we are now in the Triune God because we have been put into Him. Have we not been put into the Triune God? To be baptized is not to be baptized into Christianity, into a kind of religion, or denomination. To be baptized is to be baptized into the Triune God. The word baptize is the anglicized form of the Greek word *baptizo*. It means to drop or dip something into the water. Baptism is to be dipped, not into the water of the baptistry, but into the Triune God. Since the time we were baptized, we have been persons in the Triune God. We are in the Triune God, and we speak in the Triune God.

Those under the influence of the Pentecostal teaching may insist that to be in the Holy Spirit, one must go through a kind of "baptism in the Holy Ghost," after which he will speak in tongues. I myself was in the Pentecostal movement. I stayed with them and I joined in with them for over one year, at which time I spoke in tongues. I observed all those things. Eventually I concluded that it was a falsehood and I had to drop it. I am bold to say that today's speaking in tongues is, at least mostly, a falsehood. In the New Testament, speaking in tongues is mentioned in three books. The first mention is in Mark 16:17. The fulfillment of this verse was firstly in Acts 2. In this chapter the tongues spoken there were the different foreign dialects of the attendants who came from various parts of the world. The listeners said, "And how is it that we each hear them in our own dialect in which we were born...we hear them speaking in our tongues the great things of God (Acts 2:8, 11). This is strong proof that tongue-speaking must be an understandable language, not merely a voice or sound uttered by the tongue. The third book that speaks about tongues is 1 Corinthians. In 1 Corinthians 14:27 Paul says, "If anyone speaks in a tongue, let it be by two, or at the most three, and in turn, and let one interpret." If the tongue were not a dialect, how could anyone translate it? Some may excuse the practice of merely uttering sounds or voices by claiming that these are the "tongues of angels." However, these may rather be sounds of human manufacture. Often an interpretation will be given for such a tongue. On three different occasions the interpretation of the same tongue may be greatly different. I saw this happen. Is this not falsehood? In this kind of meeting the utterance may sometimes take the form of a prediction or prophecy. Eventually the thing predicted does not happen. I have seen prophecies of earthquakes, healings, and resurrections, yet those things never came about.

Dear saints, do not listen to this kind of teaching, but come back to the pure Bible. The pure New Testament gives us the good news, the glad tidings, the gospel, which tells us, firstly that our Triune God according to His eternal purpose became a man. This man named Jesus lived on the earth for thirty-three and a half years. Then He went to the cross and was crucified there for you and me, for all God's chosen people, and for our sins. Not only was Jesus crucified there, but within Him the Triune God was crucified on the cross. His death is all-inclusive and eternal. That all-inclusive death accomplished the eternal redemption. Then He came out of death, He resurrected, becoming a life-giving Spirit. On the day of His resurrection He came back to the disciples and breathed Himself as the life-giving Spirit into them. Then He stayed with His disciples, appearing and disappearing for forty days. He ascended to the heavens and was there for ten days. On the day of Pentecost He poured Himself out as the Spirit of power economically on His disciples who had already received the Spirit of life essentially. At that point He had accomplished His entire and full salvation. From His incarnation to His outpouring as the Spirit of power economically, was the full course of His full salvation. This is the gospel, and this gospel has become the bequest in the New Testament. The New Testament simply means a new will, a divine will made as a new covenant by the dying Christ and given as a New Testament by the resurrected Christ. In this testament God has bequeathed all these wonderful items to us. Now we have this will. Therefore, incarnation is our blessing, my portion. His human living is our portion. His death is our portion. His resurrection is our portion. His breathing of Himself as the life-giving Spirit into His disciples is our portion. His ascension is our portion. And His pouring out of Himself as the Spirit of power upon His disciples economically is also our portion. All these are our portion. When we believed in Him and received Him, we received this will and all the items in it. Now we are fully identified with Him. We are fully joined to Him. We have been baptized into Him, and this baptism gives us an organic union with the Triune God. Whatever He has gone through, becomes our history. His incarnation is ours. His living on the earth is ours. His death on the cross is ours. His resurrection is ours. His breathing of the Spirit into the disciples is ours. His ascension is ours. And His pouring out of the Spirit is ours. Whatever He has gone through is ours.

Are you crucified? Yes, we were crucified two thousand years ago. Are you in the Spirit? Yes, two thousand years ago we were put into Him. Is the Spirit in you? Yes, twenty centuries ago the Holy Spirit, the life-giving Spirit, was breathed into us already. This is the gospel. Any speaking to the contrary is not the full gospel. The full gospel comprises His incarnation, His human life on earth, His death, His resurrection, His breathing, His ascension, and His outpouring. When I believed, I received the items of the full gospel. Therefore, the life-giving Spirit is in me essentially, and the Spirit of power is upon me economically. First Peter says that the Spirit of glory and of God is resting upon us (1 Pet. 4:14).

Now you can see that we are in the Spirit and in the Triune God. Therefore, we speak in the Triune God. If I were to speak that I am so weak and not in the Spirit, I would be lying to you. I would be speaking without faith. Speak in the Holy Spirit! "No one can say, Lord Jesus, except in the Holy Spirit" (1 Cor. 12:3). We can say Lord Jesus in the Holy Spirit. Do not be troubled by the question, "Have you received the Spirit?" You should say, "Why not! I have received the Holy Spirit. I am speaking Jesus. I am speaking Christ. I am speaking 'Lord Jesus.' I speak in the Holy Spirit."

SPEAKING BY THE SPIRIT OF FAITH

In 2 Corinthians 4:13, Paul says, "And having the same spirit of faith, according to that which is written, I believed, therefore I spoke; we also believe, therefore also we speak." In the first book to the Corinthians Paul tells them to speak in the Holy Spirit. Now in the second book he says that he spoke by the spirit of faith. Christians today have paid much of attention to the speaking in the Holy Spirit in 1 Corinthians. But to my knowledge, no one has ever paid much attention to the speaking by the spirit of faith.

In verse 7 Paul speaks of the treasure in earthen vessels, the very Christ as the radiance of God who was radiated into his being. Following this he said that the putting to death of Jesus was working on the apostles, and that the life of Christ was manifested in them (v. 11). At this point he mentioned the same spirit of faith. In ancient time the psalmist had the spirit of faith (Psa. 116:10). Now they the apostles also had the spirit of faith. They believed, therefore they also spoke. What did they speak? They spoke their experience. It was not just a certain doctrine, a certain point concerning the Triune God, but the experience of the death, life, and resurrection of Christ.

Even though Paul was not speaking with his tongue, he was speaking by his pen. When he was writing, he had the spirit of faith. He wrote with boldness, with the spirit of faith. Without the spirit of faith, I may speak to you about my experience of the Lord's death, life, and resurrection in this way: "Dear saints, thank the Lord I am really not worthy, but His mercy has put me here. You know I am so weak. I want to tell you that I have been put to death quite often; I am so shameful. A number of times I was really dead. But through much suffering and much prayer, yesterday I was resurrected. Still, this morning I am so weak; probably you can realize I am even sleepy." What kind of speaking is this? In this speaking there is no spirit, no faith. If Paul were here he would say, "Dear saints, let me tell you, the putting to death of Jesus has been upon me all the day. Praise Him, His life is also manifested upon me. I say this by the spirit of faith!" This makes quite a difference. Regretably, in many of the meetings the dear ones who share speak in the former, poor way. When they speak, there is no spirit. When they speak, there is no faith.

About one hundred years ago Dean Alford wrote concerning the spirit of faith, "Not distinctly the Holy Spirit,—but still not merely a human disposition: the indwelling Holy Spirit penetrates and characterizes the whole renewed man." What is referred to here as the human disposition is actually the human spirit. Even by that time the saints did not know much about the human spirit. No writers ever spoke much about the human spirit until the beginning of this century. Mrs. Penn-Lewis in one book spoke strongly concerning the difference between the human spirit and the soul and we received much help from her. We have continued to study this and have developed it to the uttermost. Now among us even the little ones know that the Holy Spirit mingles Himself with our human spirit. The spirit here is not only the Holy Spirit but the Holy Spirit with our human spirit (Rom. 8:16).

Vincent in his word study of the New Testament followed Dean Alford, saying the same thing: "Spirit of faith: not distinctly the Holy Spirit, nor, on the other hand, a human faculty or disposition, but blending both." He used the word blending. There is a blending between the Holy Spirit and our human spirit. This is what we call the mingled spirit. We have the mingled spirit of faith.

Faith is a wonder, a miracle within us. Every genuine Christian has such a wonder, a miracle within him. No one can describe or explain it, but we do have such a thing. We have illustrated this by the action of a camera. The camera has a lens outside and film within. Opposite the camera there is scenery. Also, light is needed. When you click the shutter, the light shines onto the film. There is an exposure, and a picture is produced. This exposure describes the operation of faith. We are just like a camera. The gospel described in the New Testament is the scenery, the Holy Spirit is the heavenly light, and our spirit is the film. When you hear the speaking of the gospel once, twice, even four or five times, there is a click within you. Whatever is described in the speaking would then be in your spirit. No one could ever remove it from you. That is faith.

Now by this faith you could go everywhere to tell people that Jesus is the Savior. One may ask, "How do you know?" You just know. They do not believe it, but you believe. There is no way to drop what we have received in this way. Once this click occurs in you, it remains forever. Now wherever we go we would tell people that Jesus is the Savior: "He is living and He lives in me!" In this way you speak by the spirit of faith. In my speaking you could realize that I am so strong and very bold. Why am I so bold? I have the spirit of faith. I speak, not by my mind, but by the spirit of faith.

Faith is in our spirit, which is mingled with the Holy Spirit, not in our mind. Doubts are in our mind. This can be illustrated by the situation with an angry person. When one is angry at someone, his anger is not in his mind. The anger is in his spirit. Every angry person does not exercise his mind. If he would get into his mind and consider a little, he would not be mad. This is why when you preach the gospel, you should not stir up the person's mind. If you stir up their mind, they would not believe. You should rather induce him into the spirit. Then you can complete the transaction. When we get into our mind, faith, like anger, will be gone. In such a state I may testify, "Well, I just came here yesterday to visit the church, but a brother told me this morning you are going to have a meeting, and he asked me to give a testimony. I don't know what to say. I even don't know whether what I am going to tell you is really of the spirit or from my mind. I just don't know." This kind of testimony will kill the entire meeting. No doubt I would be speaking from my thoughtful mind. I must rather give a living testimony, testifying boldly, "Saints, hallelujah! Oh the Lord Jesus is living! I want to tell you that He is living. He lives in me. And He was so living yesterday." Then I would continue to tell you much more by the spirit of faith.

This is what the church needs for edification, for the building up. Speaking in tongues, even the genuine tongues, does not build the church (1 Cor. 14:4). What builds the church? Prophecying, that is, speaking Jesus, speaking Christ, builds up the church. So Paul said, "I would rather speak five words with my mind...than ten thousand words in a tongue." Ten thousand words in a tongue means nothing in the church meetings; but the plain words spoken by anyone by the spirit of faith and in the Holy Spirit builds the church. Therefore, we all have to practice everywhere to speak. We speak on the street; we speak in the classroom; we speak in the office; we speak at home; we speak to everybody, to all kinds of persons; and, we especially speak in the meetings, even the more in the home meetings. Learn to speak this way. This kind of speaking enlivens, this kind of speaking refreshes, this kind of speaking makes people new, this kind of speaking makes people strong and happy, and this kind of speaking imparts life to others and dispenses the Triune God into the listeners. This kind of speaking will overcome any kind of opposing environment. We must speak, speak in the Holy Spirit and speak by the spirit of faith. If everyone would become a speaker, a speaking witness, the situation would be overturned. This kind of speaking is a strong testimony of the Lord's recovery. We must not simply have a congregation with a speaker, hymns, a prayer, a speech, and so forth; we must be different. We must be revolutionized to have new meetings with everybody speaking. There should be no chairman, no one presiding. Everybody speaks everywhere, anytime, to anyone. We speak in the Holy Spirit and by the spirit of faith.

5-9-88

CHAPTER FOUR

THE DIVINE SPEAKING
WITH THE WORD OF CHRIST

Scripture Reading: Col. 3:16-17; 1 Tim. 6:3; 1 Thes. 1:8; Heb. 1:2

In prior chapters we have seen the divine speaking in God's old creation and in His new creation; the divine speaking in our daily life, ministry, and meetings; and the divine speaking in the Holy Spirit and by the spirit of faith. In this chapter we come to the divine speaking with the word of Christ.

LIVING ORGANS TO SPEAK CHRIST

To speak we surely need the word. I often have pondered on the wonderful fact that God created man with vocal chords for speaking. It is really foolish to say that there is no God. If there were no God how could we have vocal chords? If there were no God how could we have two lips and a tongue. We all know that these three members are not only for eating, they are also for speaking. Even teeth are not only for biting but also for speaking. We have vocal chords with a tongue, two lips, and many teeth for speaking. Furthermore, we not only make sounds, but we speak meaningfully, with denotation.

God created us with vocal chords, a tongue, lips, and teeth that we may be filled with Christ who is the Word of God. When we are filled with Christ as the Word of God, we speak. We speak Christ in a language such as Chinese, English, Greek, or Hebrew, not in nonsensical utterances. We speak Christ in our mother tongue. We speak Christ in our borrowed tongue. All the denotations of our speaking concentrate on one Person, Christ.

The Bible, which is called in history, The Book, concentrates on Christ. Christ is the center. Christ is the denotation. Christ is the meaning. Christ is the reality. Christ is the centrality and universality of the Book of books. "In the beginning was the Word...and the Word became flesh" (John 1:1, 14). This Word who was in the beginning is God. The Word is God. Our God is just the Word. The word is for speaking, speaking is for understanding, understanding is for believing, and believing is for receiving the Triune God as the speakable word. When we receive Christ we receive the Triune God as the word for us to speak. This word is Spirit and is life. The word is God, God is the Word, this Word is the Spirit, and this Spirit is life. All these are equivalent. The Word, God, Spirit, and life are equivalent. All are one matter. The word is good for us to speak, to understand, to receive, and to believe. Faith comes from hearing, and hearing comes from preaching, from speaking (Rom. 10:14-17). Not only is our God the speaking God, but we are the speaking beings. The wonderful thing is that today our God speaks to us and we speak to Him. We not only speak to Him, we speak Him to others. We speak Him forth, we speak for Him, and we foretell and predict concerning Him. Saints, do not forget that you have been created by God to be His speaking organ. Therefore exercise to be such a living organ.

THE WORD OF CHRIST, THE HEALTHY WORDS, AND THE WORDS OF THE LORD

In Colossians 3:16 Paul says, "Let the word of Christ dwell in you richly." The word dwell is a strong word meaning to make home, to make His home in you. Can anything which is lifeless dwell? We do not use such a predicate for a lifeless thing. Dwell is a predicate used for something living. We do not say that a bed or a nightstand dwells in our bedroom. We do not even say that our dog dwells in our bedroom. We only say a person dwells—my father dwells there, I dwell there, my wife dwells there, or my little boy dwells there. We use the word dwell only for a life with the highest person. "Let the word of Christ dwell in you" indicates that the word of Christ is a personified word that dwells as a person. Do you not believe that all the words of Christ are personified, since Christ is the Word? He is the Word of God. Phrases in the Bible such as the life of God, the light of God, the love of God, and the word of God always denote an apposition. The life of God means that life and God are one thing. God is in apposition to life. In the phrase, the love of God, love is in apposition to God. God is love and love is God. In the same way, the word of God means that God is the Word and the Word is God. In John 6:63 the Lord Jesus says, "The words which I have spoken unto you are spirit and are life." The word, the Spirit, and the life are all one thing.

Therefore, dear saints, to have the divine speaking is not a small matter. To have the divine speaking is to speak God. When you speak His word you speak God. When you speak the gospel, you speak God. When you speak the glad tidings, you speak God. When you speak grace, you speak God. This is why I use this term, the divine speaking. This is not a natural human speaking but a speaking constituted with the element of God, hence, a divine speaking. For a young boy to say that a man is made by God as His vessel to contain Him, is a divine speaking. For him to say, "You have to realize that you need Jesus; only Christ could satisfy you" is not a human speaking but a divine speaking, fully constituted with the divine elements.

In 1 Timothy 6:3 Paul speaks of some foolish ones who were not consenting to "healthy words, those of our Lord Jesus Christ." Some words in this universe are healthy, and these healthy words are of the Lord Jesus Christ. These healthy words heal, enliven, and raise people from the dead. In 1 Thessalonians 1:8 Paul says, "from you the word of the Lord has sounded out, not only in Macedonia and Achaia, but in every place your faith toward God has gone out." In these verses we have the word of Christ, the healthy words of the Lord Jesus Christ, and the word of the Lord.

THE WORD OF CHRIST BECOMING THE NEW TESTAMENT

When I studied these verses, I wondered what were the words of Christ since at Paul's time the New Testament was still being written. Firstly, the words of Christ were verbally passed on from the mouths of the apostles to others. Secondly, as the apostles did a lot of speaking in their messages, no doubt notes were taken down by the listeners. Those notes, no doubt, were passed on from one to another as the word of Christ. Thirdly, probably many early disciples wrote different gospels—not only four. The four Gospels were selected from many, perhaps from over one hundred biographies written by the early disciples. History tells us that there were a lot of writing by the early disciples, besides what was collected into the New Testament. Since most of them were not so accurate, not many of them were selected. Even by 325 A.D. when the Nicean council took place, seven books were still not recognized, not fully selected, including Hebrews and Revelation. They were not selected until 397, in the council at Carthage, North Africa. That final selection completed the entire New Testament. Those many books written by the apostles were full of the word of Christ. Hebrews 1:1-2 says that God in ancient times, in the Old Testament times, spoke through the prophets, but now in the New Testament times, God speaks in Christ. In the entire New Testament age, not only in the three and a half years of Jesus Christ's earthly life, God speaks in the Person of the Son. Today we have to realize that the Son has been made a corporate One. We the believers of His Son all have become the parts of this corporate One, a corporate Son. Therefore, God is still speaking through the Son, that is, through the church.

I believe while we are speaking here, God speaks in us. God speaks in us, because we speak the Son of God.

Now we know where are the words of Christ. Today we have the completed New Testament of twenty-seven books with many words of Christ. I hope that you dear young saints would spend some time to find out and to figure out how many words and sentences in the New Testament are the direct words spoken by the Lord Jesus. Matthew 5—7 are the direct words that came out of the mouth of the Lord Jesus. In John 14—17 are the Lord's message and prayer. These are the exact words that came out of His mouth. Spend time on these seven chapters. Consider John 17:17, "Sanctify them in the truth; Your word is truth." After your four years of study, I will give you four questions: What is to be sanctified? What is the truth? How can the word be the truth? Is the truth sanctifying you or is it the word? After speaking chapters fourteen through sixteen, the Lord looked up to the heavens and prayed, "Father, glorify Your Son that the Son may glorify You" (17:1). What does this mean? How could you explain it?

SPEAKING FOR NOURISHMENT

Do not be disappointed; be encouraged! Even if you do not understand or cannot explain these verses just say, "Father, glorify Your Son that Your Son may glorify You!" Try to say this; try to speak this in your home meeting. When five or six of us come together, you say to me, "Glorify the Son that the Son may glorify You. Father, glorify the Son." Then I respond to you, "that the Son may glorify You." If you would just speak this, you would feel nourished and you would feel sanctified! You may not know what is to be sanctified, yet you feel sanctified. Wonderful! In a good sense, you do not need to understand it. Up to the very present day, I do not know what is a detergent. But I do know when something is dirty, I wash it with detergent. Do you know everything concerning your

food? I learned the term protein, but I really do not know
what is protein. I also learned the terms B-1, B-2, B-12, and
B-complex. I learned all of this mostly from my wife. She
taught me, but neither of us really know what these are.
Yet every day she gives me vitamins, saying "This is B-2
and this is B-complex." I do not understand, I cannot
explain, but I use it, and I get it. We do not know much
about the food we eat. If you would say, "I have to study
for four years as a dietician, then I will eat," then you will
soon die. Do not wait until you understand to eat. Just eat!
Do not try to understand the Bible. The Bible is understandable, but it is not to be understood to the uttermost.
We will need eternity to know what the Bible says, yet we
can eat! We can say, "Father, glorify Your Son that the
Son may glorify You. Oh, Father, sanctify us by Your
truth; Your word is the truth." You speak it and you get it!
It is wonderful.

However, do not say this formally. Do not say it
religiously. Do not say it habitually. Say it in the Holy
Spirit, and say it by the spirit of faith: "Father, sanctify
me by Your truth; Your word is the truth." Say it this way!
Even if you do not understand it, you will get the
nourishment.

I just cannot tell you how much time I have spent on
John 14—17. But still today when I come to these four
chapters, I am just a new reader. I have written quite a few
notes on all of these chapters, but I still admit that I do not
know much. What does it mean that the Lord is the true
vine? In the Life-study of John I did tell you that this vine
is the organism of the Triune God to dispense Himself into
all the branches of this organism. Yet, I still admit that it
is hard to know these things adequately.

Therefore, dear saints, do not be bothered or disappointed; just learn to speak the word of Christ. Let the
word of Christ dwell in you. Colossians 3:16 first says, "Let
the word of Christ dwell in you richly." Then it goes on to
say "in all wisdom teaching and admonishing one another."

You teach me by the word of Christ that dwells in you, and I teach you. You admonish me and I admonish you. Furthermore it says, "in psalms and hymns and spiritual songs." In this verse the words of Christ become psalms and hymns and spiritual songs. Does this mean that the words spoken by Christ in Matthew 5—7 are all poetry? Is John 14—16 all poetry? It is possible; do not be quick to say no. I read an article which says that 1 Timothy 3:16, "Great is the mystery of godliness, who was manifested in the flesh," was a short psalm. Paul, in writing 1 Timothy, quoted that psalm. To "let the word of Christ dwell in you" and "teaching and admonishing" are not two things. Even in the English translation the grammar indicates that these are one thing. "Let the word of Christ dwell in you richly in all wisdom, teaching and admonishing." While you are letting the word of Christ dwell in you, you teach, you admonish. Yet you teach, you admonish one another not in plain words, but in psalms. Therefore, the words of Christ now are psalms, hymns, and songs.

Colossians 3:16 is a parallel portion to Ephesians 5:18-19 which says, "Be filled in spirit, speaking to one another in psalms and hymns and spiritual songs." These verses prove that when you are letting the word of Christ dwell in you, you will be filled in your spirit. In other words, when you are filled in your spirit, surely your spirit will be full of the word of Christ. The word of Christ is God, the Spirit, and the life. These four—the word, God, the Spirit, life—are synonyms. When you are filled with the word, then you are filled with God. When you are filled with God, you are filled with the Spirit. Then you are filled with life. "Let the word of Christ dwell in you," means you are being filled with God! "Do not be drunk with wine...but be filled in spirit" with God. This very God is the word of Christ, and this word of Christ is the Spirit and the life. Oh, dear saints, it is hard to explain in words, but if you consider your experience, you will say, "Amen! That's right. I

cannot explain, but I say amen!" When I let the word of
Christ dwell in me, I am just full of God, I am full of the
Spirit, I am full of life.

SPEAKING FOR DISPENSING

This filling is not only for your nourishment, it is for
you to dispense. It is for you to generate. Every human
being is made by God to propagate, to generate. Therefore,
everybody has to bring forth children! Now we all have to
learn how to generate, how to dispense, how to impart into
others what we have received into our being. This is to
reproduce, this is to generate, this is to bring forth new
Christians by speaking. Therefore, speaking is generating,
speaking is imparting, speaking is dispensing.

Let us add all these things together: speaking in the
Holy Spirit and by the spirit of faith with the word of
Christ! Where is the word of Christ? It is filling you within;
it is dwelling in you. And who is the One dwelling in you?
He is God, and God is the Spirit, not just in the heavens,
but dwelling in you. You must say, "I believe it, so I speak!
And I speak by the spirit of faith!" Christ's words dwells in
me, therefore I am full of God, Spirit, and life. This is why I
can speak to you by the spirit of faith. While I am
speaking, I am infusing, I am imparting, I am dispensing,
I am generating! I have the assurance that even some
new ones who have never heard this kind of thing,
who have never believed in the Lord Jesus, will be
regenerated while they are listening to our speaking.
Sometimes my unbelieving friends, who did not know
anything about the divine speaking, said to me "Why are
you so powerful and so attracting. How could you attract
so many, not only the Chinese, but the Americans,
Japanese, Koreans, Brazilians, Germans, British and
French." I said to them, "You may not know, but I hope
that you could be attracted also! Then you will be blessed."
It is so pleasant to be infused. If a ball were to become flat
it would feel very poor, but when it is filled with air, it

would feel so comfortable. Similarly, if you do not come to the meeting but remain at home you will feel bad, you will feel flat, not able to bounce up. If you speak when you come to the meeting, you will be filled up. If you do not speak, you will be regretful and ask, "Why didn't I speak? There was a good chance for me to speak. Why didn't I do it? Then I would have enjoyed the meeting!" I am the best enjoyer of the meetings because I speak the most! However, I should also be fair, just, and righteous to let you have some of the time. I should not rob you or occupy your time. Enjoy yourself by speaking! God spoke in His old creation and He spoke in His new creation. Now is our turn to speak in our daily life, in our ministry, in the meetings, in the Holy Spirit, by the spirit of faith, and with the word of Christ. We have the Holy Spirit in whom we can speak, we have the spirit of faith by which we can speak, and we have the word of Christ, which is God with the Spirit, which is life, with which we can speak. We have something that we can speak in, speak by, and speak with! We all can speak in the Holy Spirit, by the spirit of faith, and with the word of Christ. Now, do it! Amen!

5-9-88

CHAPTER FIVE

THE DIVINE SPEAKING WITH THE LIFE-STUDIES NOT TO REPLACE THE BIBLE BUT TO OPEN AND EXPOUND THE WORD OF GOD AND TO RELEASE ITS UNSEARCHABLE RICHES

Scripture Reading: Luke 24:27, 31-32, 44-45; Acts 8:30-35

To pay our full attention to the present move of the Lord among us, the building up of the home meetings, is absolutely scriptural. The more we come back to the New Testament to study the matter of Christian meetings, the more we are convinced that in God's intention, Christians should pay their full attention to the home meetings. It is scriptural to emphasize that we need to come back to the home meetings to set them up, establish them, and build them up.

THE HOME MEETINGS BUILDING UP THE CHURCH

In the 1930's Brother Nee told us repeatedly and insisted strongly that we should give up the Sunday morning service meeting in all the churches. He proposed that we use that time on Sunday mornings to preach the gospel to our relatives, friends, colleagues, and schoolmates. But it is hard to break people of their habit. Today people do not work on Sundays and, as a kind of custom and habit, come together as religious people to give a service to God. We are very much the same. When Brother Nee proposed this strongly, nearly no one among us paid much attention to it. Everyone was used to coming to a big morning meeting on the Lord's Day to sit and relax and listen to a good message. The good message is a kind of music which becomes people's amusement and their enjoyment. If you stop it and you ask them to preach the gospel, that means you cut off their amusement and you ask them to labor. They do not know how to preach the gospel in their homes. If they could collect their relatives, who would speak for them? Even to collect relatives is not so easy. So no one would do it, and that forced Brother Nee somewhat to let it go.

In the Far East, in the rich Chinese families, none of the family members cook, but rather they hire a professional, trained cook. At every meal time, this professional, trained cook prepares a feast for them. It is not a meal, but a feast. At noon there may be twelve dishes and sometimes at dinner, fifteen to eighteen dishes. They have a feast everyday. I lived in Shanghai for years and I saw this. The rich Chinese all got spoiled by this kind of feasting. I use this as an illustration.

The Lord's recovery is also rich. In every meeting you have a professional cook making a feast for you. Now your feast is stopped and your cook is fired. You are charged to go to the kitchen and stand in front of the hot oven. To cook in this way and to have to eat what you cook is not bad. Consider the society in any country. If the country is going to be strong, the families have to be built up. The building up of the country depends upon the families. If every family needs a professional cook, that spoils the entire country. A feast is rich, but it is not healthy. If for every meal you have a feast, you probably will not live to be sixty. Just because you have been taking in so much rich food you will die of a heart attack. If you want to avoid getting a heart attack, do not eat rich food. The more I eat plain food with no sugar, little oil, and nearly no salt, the more I feel comfortable all day. But to eat this kind of plain food is really a suffering. Likewise, to take away your big meetings to you is a suffering. That is just a suffering in taste but not the real suffering in fact, To take American desserts away from you rescues you from the upcoming heart attack. My restricted diet rescues me from committing a gradual suicide. Dear saints, do not think I am too much. Your attending the big meetings to sit there listening to a good speaker week after week, year after year, is to commit a gradual suicide.

Look at the situation in today's Christianity. The big speakers and top giants always speak, speak, speak. They gained a great number of people, but where is the real building? There is no building, yet the Lord Jesus said clearly in Matthew 16, "I will build my church upon this rock." This was a strong word, yet two thousand years have passed, and today where is the building? Through the centuries in Christianity you could only see activities, schedules, and projects, but no building. No need to say the members of Christianity, even the pastors have not been built together. It is difficult to find two famous pastors who would work together. Everyone carries out his own project. Who would work together with others? Brother Nee said that in Christianity they just shake hands over the fence. Shaking hands cannot last too long. After shaking hands, everybody goes back to their own activity. You could not see Christians who are built together.

I was a member of the Chinese Independent Presbyterian church. I was baptized there and I attended the service there for years, but I rarely talked to anyone other than the pastor. Then I joined the Brethren assembly in my town. I went to their meetings five times a week for seven and a half years but I scarcely talked to anybody. In such a meeting there was little contact with others.

In Matthew 16:18 the Lord said that He would build His church upon the rock of the revelation concerning Christ. Then in chapter eighteen the Lord Jesus said that He is in the midst wherever or whenever two or three are gathered into His name (v. 20). In this verse the Greek preposition *eis*, translated "into", indicates that these two or three who are gathered into the name of Christ are gathered out of themselves into His name. The name always denotes a person. These two or three are gathered out of themselves into the Person of Jesus Christ. Here they meet together.

In such a small meeting, how could you avoid the contact with others. When you meet in a gathering of five hundred it is hard for you to speak and easy for you not to speak. But when you meet with just one other person you cannot avoid speaking. Let me illustrate the speaking that might take place in such a small meeting. Perhaps one brother may say that he does not know how to speak and that he does not have anything to speak. He does not like to read the life-study message, nor does he like to read the Bible. The other brother may tell him, "Years ago I did not like the Bible either, but now I like it very much. I did not like it in the past, because I did not have the appetite. Then one day I regretted and repented of my lack of appetite for the Bible. I had a thorough confession of my sins before the Lord. After that I was so happy that I was filled. I jumped, I laughed, and I exulted. Since that time I have loved the Bible and I have the appetite for the Bible." Then he may help the first brother to receive grace by confessing. This is building up. The first brother will become thankful to the Lord and grateful to this brother. He will never forget him, and he will love him. This kind of experience builds us together.

Then these brothers may fellowship about how enjoyable it is to come together in this way. Perhaps one brother may express a concern for brothers that do not come to their meeting. They may pray with tears, "Lord, have mercy upon Dave, have mercy upon Don, have mercy upon James." By this kind of prayer these two brothers love each other and get into each other's heart. They are built together. This kind of building together will impress people

to the uttermost. Then the two would go to see the
backsliding brother. This brother may know that the two
were not one in the past, but now he sees that they are so
one. There is hardly any need for them to say anything. He
would be impressed and inspired. It is so easy to recover
him. Gradually day after day this one and that one will be
recovered. These small meetings will build up the saints,
keep the saints, recover the backsliding ones, and also
bring in the new ones.

Those who are accustomed to the enjoyment of the big
meetings have to realize that the big meetings can never
build up. In Taiwan after 1960 we slowly and unconsciously
drifted back to the way of Christianity. Gradually we gave
up the practice of the small groups. Although year after
year we baptized more than eight hundred, eventually not
many were preserved. We did not have the preserving
strength. We did not have a proper reservoir to keep the
rain because we did not practice the home meetings. We
had strong Sunday morning meetings in some halls, but
that did not fulfill the purpose of building. So we surely
discovered the shortage, the need of the home meetings. We
have to endeavor, struggle, and strive for the building up
of the home meetings.

To turn our attention from big meetings to small
meetings may temporarily be a kind of suffering, but for
the long run it will be a very healthy activity in the Lord's
recovery. We are not accustomed to having small meetings
in the homes. We like to have the big meetings. We even
pray for big speakers. That means we want a big cook to
come, to cook feasts for us. But to eat feasts every day is
not healthy. The most healthy way is to eat home-cooked
meals. Home cooking is really healthy. Everyone can live a
long life by eating home meals. Even if they never have
one feast in their whole life, still they will be healthy. But I
assure you, if every day you attend a feast, you will soon
die.

A big feast is tasteful, but for the long run it is not

healthy. Big meetings are tasteful and enjoyable, but for the long run they do not build up the Body of Christ. Occasionally, we may all come together for a big feast like the Israelites in the ancient time. They stayed home and ate their home meals for nearly the whole year. Only three times a year they all came together to have a feast lasting not more than seven days. This is very good, but after this you have to go back to your home meals to make you healthy. Learn to treasure the small meetings. Even if you do not feel so tasteful as in the big meetings, try to enjoy it. Try to talk with some new ones or with some who are weaker, who have been away from the church meetings for a while. Try to talk to them. This will help the building.

THE PURPOSE OF THE LIFE-STUDIES

Now let us come to the divine speaking with the Life-studies. In the past some have had the thought that we use the Life-studies in our meetings to replace the Bible. But we do not replace the Bible by anything, even by using the Life-studies. Rather, I must say honestly, and you have to admit the fact, no book ushers us into the Bible as the Life-studies do. Anyone can prove and can testify how much we love the Bible, how much we pay our attention to the Bible, and how much we get ourselves into the Bible through the study of the Life-studies.

So the Life-studies are not to replace the Bible, but to open the Bible and to expound the Bible and to release all the unsearchable riches in the Bible. Quite a few in the past came to me to express how the Life-studies opened the Bible and helped them to know the Bible. After I got saved at close to twenty years of age, I began to study the New Testament. I got stuck on the first page. I wondered, "Who is Abraham?" I got a lexicon which told me that Abraham was the father of Isaac. Then when I looked up Isaac it just said that Isaac was the son of Abraham. After that, whenever I came back to Matthew I just skipped the first seventeen verses. I would not read that portion on the

genealogy of Christ. There were too many names I did not
know how to pronounce. It seemed impossible for me to
understand, and I thought to myself, "Probably there's no
one on this earth who knows this portion."

But today if you have trouble with the first seventeen
verses of Matthew chapter one, you can go to the Life-
study of Matthew. There are seven messages on the
genealogy of Christ. Those messages open up this portion
and expound its full significance to you. They also release
all the riches. In the summer of 1936 I was able to write an
article which was published as a book in Chinese entitled
The Gleanings of the Genealogy of Christ. The messages I
gave in the Life-study of Matthew on chapter one were all
based upon that article. Now that portion is fully opened
and expounded and all the riches are released now in black
and white. This is not to replace Matthew 1; this is to open
up that difficult section of the Word with a full exposition
and with a rich presentation of all its unsearchable riches.
This is the use of the Life-studies.

For the six chapters of Ephesians we put out ninety-
seven Life-study Messages. Ephesians contains a lot of
deep, profound, spiritual terminology. How could you
understand what is the glory of God's inheritance in the
saints? And what is glory? It is difficult. I have been
spending years to study the text, to study the Greek text, to
study some expositions, and to study to know the Bible by
experience. Through many years of study and observation
I surely got an accumulation.

The Bible has been in the hands of Christians for over
nineteen centuries. A number of great scholars have
studied and expounded this book. Following the lead of
Brother Watchman Nee, some of us have read and become
familiar with all the great writers' masterpieces. The Life-
study Messages are now just the cream of the milk
produced in nineteen centuries. I presented them in a very
simple way and in very plain English.

All of my writings have been polished by the American

brothers and sisters because English is not my native tongue. Sometimes in their polishing they added in some deeper words. When I made the final review I always took away all the deeper words added by them. Whether the word is deep or shallow, as long as it conveys the thought to people, that is good enough. I like for people to be able to read my writings without a dictionary. Right away they can understand what the black and white says. Then the Holy Spirit has a way to work within them. If you use language that is too deep or too profound, their mind might be fully occupied just with the language. This leaves no capacity in their mind to understand the spiritual denotations or the spiritual significances. Such a thing is absolutely wrong. The language in the Gospel of John is so simple: "In the beginning was the Word"; "I am the light of the world"; "I am the bread of life." Probably even some in kindergarten today could read John. The denotation, the significance, is very profound, but the language does not bother people. The language does not occupy people's mentality. This is the way we have taken with the Life-studies. They are written in a very simple and plain way with the intention to open the Bible.

I believe if you do have a heart to read any book of the New Testament with the help of the Life-studies, right away that book would be opened to you. This is what the Lord Jesus did in Luke 24. Firstly, He opened the Scriptures (v. 32), then He opened their mind to understand the Scriptures (v. 45). The Scriptures were altogether closed to the disciples. In the Pentateuch, in the Psalms, and in the Prophets there are many things concerning Christ, but none of the disciples saw anything. Why was this? It was because the Scriptures were not opened to them and their spiritual understanding was not opened. So the Lord Jesus came to the two disciples going down to Emmaus. They saw Him, but they did not recognize Him until they sat to eat with Him. Once their eyes were opened, Jesus disappeared from their sight. They said to one another, "Was not our heart burning within us while He was speaking to us on the road, while He was opening to us the Scriptures?" (v. 32). Then they turned to go back to Jerusalem. There the Lord Jesus appeared to them again and opened their understanding to realize what is mentioned in the law of Moses, in the Psalms, and in the Prophets concerning Christ. The purpose of the life-studies is just to open up the Bible.

Another example of the opening of the Bible is found in Acts 8. As Philip the evangelist was traveling, the Spirit told him to go and join the chariot of an Ethiopian eunuch. The eunuch was reading the passage of Scripture in Isaiah 53. When Philip asked him, whether he understood what he read, the eunuch answered, "How can I unless someone guides me?" So Philip explained to him the significance of what was spoken in Isaiah, that Jesus Christ as the Lamb was slaughtered for our sins. That was a real gospel. Right away the eunuch believed and was baptized. Without the help of such a guide when you open up some of the books of the New Testament, it is really hard for you to understand.

Readers of the New Testament have found at least fifty points that are very difficult for people to understand. In the Life-studies I solved each one of these major problems. For instance, after Jesus was buried in the tomb He went to the spirits in prison. What was that? There are many different explanations, but after much study, I came to a conclusion and wrote an adequate note on this matter (1 Peter 3:19 and note 19[2]). When you come to any book in the New Testament with the help of the Life-study, you will have no problem with the difficult points.

The main purpose of the Life-study is to minister life. This is why I call it a Life-study. In history this term has never been used. No one has ever called their study of the New Testament a Life-study. Actually it is a study that concerns life only. These Life-studies are not intended to pass on mere knowledge to you. There is some amount of knowledge, but I purposely limited it. The main purpose is to minister life. I have received many letters expressing appreciation for the Life-studies. These letters testified that every page and every paragraph supplied life. Many good books are just like a deep mine; you need to read through eight pages before you get one diamond. But the Life-studies have a diamond within the first half of a page. It seems I am boasting. Actually I am not boasting, I am speaking the fact.

THE USE OF THE LIFE-STUDIES IN THE HOME MEETINGS

I am burdened concerning how we use the Life-studies in the home meetings. In the past some have selected a good speaker and charged him to read a Life-study several times and to remember all the crucial points of the message. On Sunday morning the speaker came to the platform to speak this message. Because this way has not always been so successful, some have changed their way. They asked all the saints to read the Life-study before coming to the meeting. In the meeting one or two would take the lead to have some read a paragraph at a time. After the reading of a paragraph there was the opportunity to speak if anyone was inspired. Eventually, this way was not successful either. So some tried to read selected portions of the Life-study in the meeting to see if there was an inspiration from the aggregate of several sections. This way also became a failure. Eventually nearly all the churches do not know how to use the Life-study Messages in the meetings. They all know that diamonds, jewels, and jade are here in the Life-studies, but they do not know how to use them.

In Hong Kong those that sell diamonds are trained to be able to present a diamond from many angles. They can explain everything about a diamond in such a way that the customers are attracted, showing it to them from many angles, and explaining everything. With this explanantion half of the listeners get attracted, asking "How much? Let

me see it." Those salesmen were trained. They surely know
salesmanship. But we are not like this. We do not know
how to show the angles of the diamond. We do not even
know the difference between a diamond and jade. We have
all the precious stones, yet we do not know how to use
them. This has forced me to consider the situation.
Sometimes I could not sleep so well at night just
considering this matter of how to use the Life-studies.

We should use the Life-studies, but not in all those other
ways. Forget about all those ways. We should use the Life-
studies in the small meetings. Let the saints know that we
are going to use a certain message of the Life-study as the
very material for our speaking in the meeting. Then when
we all come to the meeting, we will begin to read it. There
are at least seven ways to read. First, you have to read in a
short way. Just read a short portion. Sometimes you do not
need to read a full sentence, because you may realize that a
phrase or a clause is crucial. For instance, you may read,
"But when it pleased God...to reveal His Son in me" (Gal.
1:15a, 16a). When you read this, you could surely realize
that this is not a common word; this is too crucial.
Therefore, you should not read ahead too quickly. You
have to linger for a while: "It pleased God to reveal His
Son in me." When you pause, some others will repeat it.
First, you read a short portion. Second, if that portion is
crucial, repeat it. But do not repeat it in a formal way. We
must repeat in a living way, not in a dead or formal way.
This repeating-reading is very living, very meaningful,
and very impressing. "It pleased! It pleased God to reveal
His Son in me!"

A third way is to read with some explanation, but not
with too much. Sometimes some wordings or terminologies
in certain messages are not common. People just do not
know the meaning of them. For instance, Matthew 1:21
says, "You shall call His name Jesus." You may repeat,
"Jesus! Jesus!" But nobody knows what Jesus means. You
have the repetition, but there is the need of some

explanation: "Call His name Jesus. Call Him Jehovah the Savior." Read it in an explaining way. In your reading, you will give people the meaning. Sometimes you may feel this explanation is good and worthy of repetition. Then you would say, "Jesus, Jehovah the Savior. Oh, Jehovah the Savior!" This impresses people. This way requires a lot of learning. Therefore we all have to learn. Especially in this age, in the twentieth century, everything requires a lot of learning. To be a twentieth century believer in the Lord's recovery, you cannot be too simple.

Another way is to pray-read. Sometimes when you have crucial verses, you have to pray-read them. When you read these verses, you realize that they are crucial and that they should be repeated. After one reads, right away you repeat. This is to pray-read. You also need to read with some variation in your voice, just like music. Sometimes the melody goes up and comes down. Sometimes it is faster; sometimes it is slower. Sometimes you have to read loudly, and sometimes you have to read not so loud. We have to learn this. We are not machines. We are not robots. We are very living. We know how to lift up our voice, and how to lower it down. We all have to learn the proper way. We have a sober mind and we have a spirit. We just exercise our spirit, and we know when is the time to utter something. We also know how long we should utter it and how much we should say.

To open up the home meetings may afford some who like to speak a good chance to occupy the entire time with their speaking. This is a real concern. I beg you all, for love's sake—we all love the Lord, we all love His Body, we all love His church—for the sake of this love, we all have to function properly. Do not occupy others' time. Do not speak too long; do not speak too much; do not pray too long. We all have to learn this. Then we could practice using the Life-studies in a good way.

We can also pray-sing. When we read a verse, perhaps you will have a hymn or a chorus that just matches that thought. For instance, Galatians 2:20 says, "It is no longer I who live, but Christ lives in me." There is a hymn with just such a chorus, "Christ lives in me, Christ lives in me." When you read, "No longer I, but Christ lives in me," right away someone may take the lead to sing that chorus, "Christ lives in me, Christ lives in me." This is why I call it pray-singing.

Then, there is another way to read: to read in order to apply, an applying-reading. You may read a verse, and apply this verse to your situation, to your present need. There are more ways of reading. It is not limited. We all have to be living, open, flexible, and adjustable. Let us all try and learn. We are all still in the learning stage. The best place for you to practice this learning is in the home meetings.

Recently I attended a small home meeting in Taipei. At first I was disappointed. By the scheduled time of meeting there were only an old man, a small girl, and a young schoolteacher. Slowly others came in. Eventually a backsliding brother took the lead to speak a gospel hymn. A sister played the piano and all began to sing the hymn. Afterwards the backsliding one gave an explanation of the whole hymn. By the end of the meeting I was very encouraged. This proves that the home meetings really work. They bring in the backsliders and make them the leaders. They bring in the people from the denominations and bring in the new converts. They bring in many different people, and eventually everybody feels happy. However there is still one problem. Many still do not know how to use the Life-studies.

We need to use the Life-studies in order to enrich the home meetings, to strengthen the home meetings, to refresh, and to make them so alive, so attractive, even so attracting, and so upholding. I believe we will reach this goal. If we would endeavor, we will surely reach the goal, and the churches will all be built up. Once the churches are built up, the increase will surely come in. If we all begin to speak, the Lord will honor our speaking. Sooner or later, this one will be saved, that one will be saved; there will be some saved here and there. All these saved ones will be brought in. This is the way!

5-9-88